To Louise Johns Photography for the beautiful cover photograph of Chaka

To the many friends and family for the extraordinary love, support and
encouragement we have received

To everyone who provided photos for use in the book

To Brent, Alison Wilhelmi and Randi Tonnesson
for the extra eyes and editorial advice

To Blue Fox Press for their belief in "The Story of Chakadog and his Human"
and for all of the support in getting this story out

First Printing, 2017

ISBN 978-1-943880-17-1
Library of Congress Control Number 2017953886

BlueFox Press
2825 E. Cottonwood Pkwy. Suite 500
Salt Lake City, UT 84121

Bluefoxpress.com

an imprint of
BlueFox Press

The Story of
Chakadog & His Human

The pit bull and his "human" young man.
They loved each other unconditionally and forever.

Debby Turkington, Author

Once upon a time, not so very long ago, a sweet, cute pit bull puppy was born. He was brown and white and everyone said he had the most beautiful eyes. Some humans believe that all pit bull puppies will grow up to be mean or dangerous. This particular, little puppy certainly wasn't either. He wanted to adopt a human who understood that, so he passed over a lot of humans before he chose his forever one.

But, boy oh boy, when he finally found the right human, it was wonderful, obviously meant to be and it lasted forever.

The puppy's human wanted to find a name that was both strong and kind for his sweet puppy boy. He finally decided that Chaka was the perfect name...and so it was. The first thing his human did was to remove the chain collar Chaka wore around his neck and bought a new soft, but strong collar that didn't hurt Chaka's little neck.

His human brought Chaka to live in a small town where his human's family and his two sister dogs, Maggie and Kira lived. Everybody (well, practically everybody and their dog) in the small town came to know and love Chakadog (as he was affectionately called). He was such a good dog. He was polite and kind. He didn't bark at other people or dogs. He never ate another dog's food and he always seemed to be smiling. He loved his life with his human and his dog friends.

His human was an adventurous spirit who liked to do all kinds of interesting things.

Happily, near the town where Chakadog and his human lived there were many choices of fun things to do. And Chakadog almost always got to go along to join in the fun.

Chakadog and his human went everywhere together. They told each other secrets, they laughed together and cried together and they went on great adventures together.... oh what a life Chakadog and his human had!

He and Maggie and Kira learned to keep up as his human and his human's friends and their dogs, like Gracie, skied and snowboarded. Sometimes Chakadog was even in front.

He hiked and climbed mountains with his human.
He kayaked and rafted with his human.

I Love My Dog

Bon Apetit

Once Chakadog was even belayed (that means lifted) to the top of a mountain and then lowered again with the help of his special harness. Had he known exactly what that meant when his human was explaining it to him, Chakadog probably would not have been so excited to try it.

He played in rivers and helped his human catch fish. He could cliff jump into a river or lake, though, truth be told, Chakadog didn't like doing that all that much either. Thankfully, he was not allowed to go skydiving or fly the glider with his human. But Chakadog's very favorite thing in the whole world was going on camping trips and long car rides with his human, his human's friends and his dog friends.

Chakadog saved his human from a house fire once and his human saved him from all things scary (except for the belaying and cliff jumping, of course). He learned that there were certain doors that he could open so he could let himself out. Sometimes that came in handy and sometimes it got Chakadog and Marley in trouble. He was a little shy and really didn't like for humans to watch him eat, although his manners were really quite good. All in all, he was a very, very good dog who loved his human as only a dog can.

But, no matter where he was or what he was doing, whenever Chakadog heard his human's special, low, soft whistle he would listen intently and then come running with a smile that covered his whole face. It was such a soft, low whistle that most humans wouldn't even notice and it was like no other whistle most humans had ever heard. It was his human's and Chakadog's own special whistle. The one that only they knew.

After several years, Chakadog had grown big and strong. It was then that he and his human started a new adventure. The camper van was loaded and they moved from their little town far, far away to another small, but different town.

They made many new friends and did more of the things they had always loved to do. They found new things that they learned to love as well. The mountains were bigger and better, the rivers faster and colder, the fish more plentiful and lots and lots of room to do it all. Chakadog and his human learned about bears and other wild animals. But, Chakadog's human made sure they were always prepared for whatever adventures they went on.

Sometimes Chakadog had to stay home (though he never really wanted to) until his human was sure that new adventures were safe for him.

His human loved him so. And Chakadog loved his human just as much. That is why Chakadog was so very happy when his human found a human for himself.

She enjoyed the same kinds of adventures that he and his human did. Soon the three of them were always together. Life was GRAND!!

His humans had friends and their friends had dogs, like Bastion and Dexter who became Chakadog's friends. His human's human (kind of his human mom now) loved him and cared for him almost as much as his human did. They became their own little family. While his humans and their friends had to go to work sometimes, there seemed always to be time for playing and snuggling and jumping in the slur and stealing bones and just being happy. Chakadog and his human were so, so very happy.

One day, after work, Chakadog's human explained that Chakadog needed to stay home for a bit while his human and some friends went to check out a new adventure. Chakadog waited and waited for his human to come home.

And then he waited some more.
And then he waited even more,
but his human did not come home.

Chakadog was happy and relieved when he saw his human mom coming. She stayed right next to him through the night. She hugged him and kissed him and told him stories of all of the fun things he and his human had done; of all of their good times together.

His human mom cried and Chakadog knew something wasn't right. One of his human's friends stayed with them and he gave Chakadog steak for dinner... he for sure knew then that something was wrong...he hardly ever got steak. Even though that was exciting, Chakadog knew that something bad had happened and that things would never be the same for him.

Although he still got up in the mornings and took walks and hikes and sometimes played by the river, it was not the same... his human was gone. His human mom took very good care of Chakadog and loved him with all of her heart.

He tried very hard to take care of her too. He gave her kisses and snuggled with her whenever she looked sad. They were still a family, but now just two. The days went by and Chakadog got older. He and his human mom went on shorter adventures and road trips. He continued to think about the day when he and his human would be together again.

Then one day a new human found Chakadog's human mom and they fell in love. Chakadog, his human mom and her new human and his dog became a sort of second family. They all loved each other and went on adventures together. Not the same adventures (no cliff jumping) as he had gone on with **his** human, but adventures nonetheless. They even took Chakadog back to his human's favorite places in the whole, wide world, Bowman Lake and Polebridge. He thought he might find his human there. But though he searched, Chakadog could not find his human. Chakadog missed his human every day, but he was very, very glad that his human mom had found someone to make her smile again and that he had a dog brother, Huck, to snuggle with at night.

He was content.

In the Fall, Chakadog and his new family moved so that his human mom could go back to school...she's very smart. Chakadog thought he might find his human there. His family went for walks and liked their new home, but he still could not find his human. Chakadog would have liked to have been outside more. Missing his human sometimes made him really, really sad and tired. He wondered more often about how it would be when he found his human again. He would have liked to have been able to go on more adventures, but he was getting older. It was getting harder and harder for him to do the things he enjoyed. His human mom and new family took very good care of Chakadog. They took him on car rides and short hikes and made him comfortable. He was happiest when his human mom cuddled and snuggled with him, but he loved cuddling with his new dog brother, Huck, too.

One night Chakadog and his dog brother, Huck, were napping by the sofa when he thought he heard a familiar sound. He listened and heard it again. And then again. Yes, it was his human whistling for him. Chakadog wanted to get up, but his tired body didn't seem to be able to move. He so wanted to run to his human, but even if he could have, he couldn't see any way to get to his human. He listened and listened. He continued to hear the low, soft whistle throughout the night.

His human was calling Chakadog
to come be with him again.

In the morning Chakadog's family took him to the dog doctor to see why he couldn't get up. The dog doctor said that Chakadog was old and that it was indeed time for him to join his human. Chakadog's human mom asked if he could please stay for just a little bit longer. His family took Chakadog for one last, long car ride in the woods. His human mom gave Chakadog his favorite dinner, bacon. He really, really wanted to eat the bacon, but he just didn't have the energy. He was held and cuddled and slept surrounded by love from his family all night long.

In the morning light, Chakadog found that he could see the path that he just knew would lead him to his human so that they could be together forever. His human mom wrapped him in a shirt that his human had often worn. With the shirt wrapped around him, Chakadog could actually smell his human again. His human mom gave him the best of hugs and the best of kisses and then whispered in his ear "Listen for the whistle, follow the whistle, Tyler and a great new adventure will be at the end of the whistle".

And that is what Chakadog did.
He followed the whistle... one more time.

Oh, What a reunion it must have been.
Chakadog and his human together again.

I wish I could have seen it with my very own eyes.
The licking, the tickling, the laughter and tears.
I'm sure Heaven hasn't seen such a celebration in years.

Chaka, a pit bull puppy, abandoned simply because he was a pit bull, had a most incredible, long, happy, fulfilled dog life because one human didn't listen to the words of others (including, at first, his family). He and this particular puppy saw the love and kindness in each other's eyes and they both found their forever friend. Most anyone who knew Chakadog will tell you that he was, till the end, the most gentle, sweet (if sometimes stubborn—got that from his human, I'm afraid) loving dog you will ever meet. He had personality, curiosity and a zest for life—just like his human.

Tyler (Chaka's human) believed more in the goodness he saw and felt in Chaka's eyes than in what others might have thought. And Chaka did the same with Tyler. Their belief in each other was returned tenfold, a million fold.

Losing a loved one is never easy. It is devastating and sometimes simply incomprehensible to lose someone suddenly and unexpectedly. Do pets, dogs, cats, chinchillas feel the same loss and emptiness that we, as humans do? I believe so. They go on with their normal lives (which are no longer normal at all) just like we do.

The expectation of one day having a reunion of giant proportions with all my loved ones—animal and human alike, brings a measure of comfort and for a time, peace for me. Hopefully when the time comes we will all hear the whistle (in whatever form) of loved ones gone before.

Chakadog's sister dog, Kira, crossed the rainbow bridge about six months before Tyler's accident and a year and a half before Chaka. They are missed more profoundly than my meager words can express. But they are together again only missing sister dog, Maggie, who may not be far behind, brother dog, Simba, new brother dog, Huck and Smokey, the chinchilla.

As Tyler's brother said, "Kira had to go ahead so she could be there when Tyler got there, and Chaka has to stay behind until we are all ok." Apparently, Tyler believes we are all ok. Not the same, but mostly ok. So it was time he called his forever friend to be with him again.

In order to help the effort to promote education about the Pit Bull breed, a portion of the proceeds from the sale of this book will go to Nuzzles & Co. A non-profit no-kill pet rescue and adoption organization in Park City, Utah.

You may also go to nuzzlesandco.org to make a donation.

While I'm sure that this list is incomplete, our family would like to thank all of the animals (and their humans) who were such a large part of Chaka's life.

Marley
Maggie and Kira
Smokey
Simba
Gracie
Ruby
Dexter
Bastion
And many more

Finally, last but not least Huck & his family. They loved and cared for Chaka as Tyler, himself, would have had he been here. They made Chaka's last days and months the best that they could be. We are all more grateful for that than words can adequately express.

Chaka and his human, part of the landscape forever

CPSIA information can be obtained
at www.ICGtesting.com
Printed in the USA
BVOW05*1224051117
499563BV00031B/254/P